V2 CLASS
GREEN ARROWS

C.J. Freezer

Foulis

Haynes

ISBN 0 85429 427 9

A FOULIS Railway Book

First Published 1984

© **Winchmore Publishing Services Limited**

Published by:
Haynes Publishing Group
Sparkford, Yeovil,
Somerset BA22 7JJ

Distributed in USA by:
Haynes Publications Inc.
861 Lawrence Drive,
Newbury Park,
California 91320, USA

Produced by:
Winchmore Publishing Services Limited,
40 Triton Square,
London NW1 3HG

Printed in Spain by
by Graficromo s.a.

Titles in the *Super Profile* series:

Further titles in this series will be published at regular intervals. For information on new titles please contact your bookseller or write to the publisher.

Contents

Gresley and the LNER

The London and North Eastern Railway was formed on 1 January 1923 from a number of separate constituent lines. Many years before, three of them, the Great Northern, the Great Eastern and the Great Central, had attempted to amalgamate. They were thwarted by the Will of Parliament which, several elections and one world war later, decided that they were to be run together, with – to name only the other major partners – the North Eastern, the Hull and Barnsley, the North British and the Great North of Scotland.

The main underlying reason for the amalgamations of 1922–3 was that they were a sort of half-way house to nationalisation. The railways had been brought together under Government control at the outbreak of war, and there were many politicians, Liberals as well as Socialists, who wanted this control to continue. The ruling Tories were not willing to concede so fundamental a point, although the parlous financial condition of many of the railways clearly showed that something needed to be done. The result was a regional grouping of lines which lumped together the hopelessly bankrupt with the more successful, viable railways, with a view to cross-subsidy.

The two southern groups came off the best, the GWR indeed was left almost intact, whilst the three lines that went to form the Southern were in reasonable order and offered good prospects. The Northern pair did not fare so well because they had to carry the Scottish lines. The initial scheme for five groups, one exclusively Scottish, was abandoned since the most optimistic prognosis revealed that as a whole, the Scottish railways were not viable.

The West Coast group was formed from the prosperous and viable LNWR and Midland lines, with the Lancashire and Yorkshire thrown in for good measure. The Scottish Caledonian line, probably the best bet amongst the Scottish lines, was also added, and if the Highland was to be a financial burden, at least the Glasgow & South Western was not liable to lose too much money.

The LNER fared worst of all. It not only collected the 'Second Division' in Scotland but its English constituents were also in financial difficulties. The Great Central had always been a liability, the Great Eastern had had to fight to become reasonably prosperous, and the North Eastern, once the most solidly based of all British companies, served a region which was already in decline. Only the Great Northern was in good financial shape.

The LNER, however, succeeded rather better than the other groups in welding the disparate parts into a whole. There was not an inherent rivalry between routes, as existed on the LMS, but the LNER management was able to retain the pride in the old companies and transform it into a greater pride in the new organisa-tion. In contrast, the LMS organisation in the first decade tended to exacerbate the old rivalry between the Midland and the LNWR, and the GSWR with the Caledonian.

A potential source of conflict was the appointment of the Chief Mechanical Engineer. This post is not the most important on the railway, since it is the traffic department that determines how the trains will run and how well they serve the public. However, the locomotive, particularly the steam locomotive, is in the public eye the most important part of the whole system, and this means that the personality and ideas of the CME are a very important factor in a company's image.

With several good men to choose from, the board opted for seniority, a sound enough prin-ciple in general since it is calcu-lated to cause least resentment. However, the senior CME of the Great Central, J. G. Robinson, was near to retirement and not only declined the post, but nominated in his place the rela-tively young CME of the Great Northern Railway, H. N. Gresley. The board concurred and events were to prove them right.

This did not mean that there was unanimous support. With the limitation of hindsight it is diffi-cult to appreciate that in 1922 Gresley was just another com-petent mechanical engineer.

Moreover, he was a man with a few odd ideas, in particular a penchant for three-cylinder drive with complicated conjugated valve gear. Although his locomotives were quite impressive, and his ideas on coaching stock sound, there was still a small question mark over him. Many men on other constituents were resentful of his promotion. This was to have its effects in later years.

However it must be understood that a CME was not omnipotent. His job was to organise all mechanical departments of the railway and, although to the enthusiast the locomotives are the most glamorous aspect of his work, there are many other equally

important areas which fell into his department. Furthermore, he did not have unlimited funds. Many commentators point out that a straightforward but costly modification might well have turned a competent but unenterprising design into a masterpiece. No doubt the CME was even more aware what could be done given the money, but for sound commercial reasons let things ride.

This needs to be fully understood, for Gresley has frequently been accused of reluctance to alter designs, as if he resented any suggestion that his original ideas were less than perfect. It is perhaps more accurate to say that time and time again, Gresley showed a marked reluctance even

Left: No 4788 under construction at Darlington, 1937.
Above: V.2 *Green Arrow* with the originally proposed number 637 in June 1936 and as No 4771.

to propose additional expenditure to the board if the existing equipment was capable of doing its job. There is an old engineering maxim, 'if it works, leave it alone'. This is valid even if an improvement is possible. There were other areas on the LNER where the same effort applied to existing equipment that was inefficient frequently paid better dividends. This was done time and time again. There is little doubt that H. N. Gresley was remarkably good at organising limited resources to produce outstanding results.

3

39

4

3695

34

29

32

33

30

26

28

27

24

35

4'0"

9'3"

8'3"

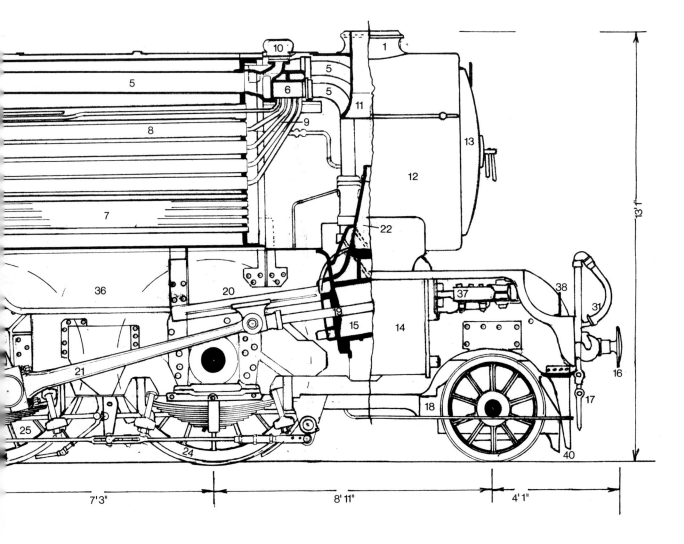

13'1"

7'3" 8'11" 4'1"

1	Chimney
2	Steam collector dome
3	Ross 'Pop' safety valves
4	Boiler casing
5	Steam pipes
6	Superheater header
7	Fire tubes
8	Superheater tubes
9	Superheater elements
10	Anti-vacuum valve
11	Petticoat pipe
12	Smokebox
13	Smokebox door
14	Outer cylinders
15	Inner cylinder
16	Buffers
17	Coupling hook
18	Pony truck
19	Piston rod
20	Slide bar
21	Connecting rod
22	Blast pipe
23	Crank arm balance weight
24	Driving wheels
25	Springs
26	Brake cylinder
27	Brake rods
28	Coupling rod
29	Firebox
30	Trailing wheel axlebox
31	Vacuum brake connection
32	Firebars
33	Ashpan
34	Driving cab
35	Trailing wheel
36	Main frame
37	Conjugating valve gear
38	Lamp brackets
39	Handrail
40	Guard irons

A 'big engine' policy?

It is often suggested that Gresley pursued a 'big engine' policy. However, any careful study of the designs brought out under his rule will show that he was responsible for a large number of quite small machines. Furthermore, if one looks at the duties the locomotives were expected to perform, none were particularly large by contemporary world standards.

One of the oddities of British steam locomotive practice in general was the tendency to produce the smallest locomotive that could do the job. Only two railways went against the trend, the Great Western and the Great Northern. However, they did not have a big engine policy as such, but a policy of providing locomotives which had some margin in hand. Such locomotives could cope with future traffic growth and, more importantly, provide the operating department with a little extra time in hand on even the most demanding of schedules so that in the event of any extra burden, the driver could cope. This could take the form of a coach or two added to the standard formation, or a succession of permanent way or signalling slacks which prevented the train from reaching the speeds and the intermediate timings laid down by the timetable compilers. But the important thing was that the train should arrive at its destination as nearly on time as possible.

This had long been accepted on the GNR, and the principle was well established that on a steam locomotive the boiler-firebox combination was the key to the problem. Doncaster Works had known for a long time that a relatively large boiler with ample heating surface and a large fire-grate was the prime requisite for a successful locomotive. No GNR design was ever seriously 'over cylindered' (the peculiar phrase coined in Victorian times to describe a design where the boiler was totally inadequate to supply the cylinders when the locomotive was opened up) a phrase which served to disguise the fact that the boiler proportions were wrong, and which often led to the cylinders being linered, rather than the boiler being improved.

This called for more than a large boiler, it also needed a large firebox. The GNR, before Gresley went over to the so-called 'wide firebox', had long favoured a large firegrate for its principal express locomotives. Although the Gresley design has been frequently termed a 'Wooten' firebox, it is not so. The Wooten, an American design, is substantially different. The true predecessor of the wide firebox fitted to the second series of GNR Atlantics was that fitted to the GWR broad gauge single drivers. However, a design built to fit the more generous space between the frames of a 7 ft (2.1 m) gauge locomotive and adapted to the narrower confines of a standard gauge chassis, led to a very significant alteration in the arrangement of the locomotives. Not that all Gresley locomotives had a wide firebox. Many were of necessity fitted with the normal narrow box that slid in between the main frames and driving wheels.

A more important feature of Gresley design was the drive itself. Except where he adapted an existing pre-grouping design to modern conditions, Gresley adopted three-cylinder propulsion, coupled with a special conjugated valve gear and high-tensile steel motion. There were several reasons for this decision.

Green Arrow class V.2 with BR No 60919 in March 1963, near Perth.

LNER class V.2 No 4795 soon after its entry into service in 1938.

Firstly, on the largest and most powerful locomotive then being produced, the power output was beginning to demand more than two cylinders.

Secondly, there was the problem of 'hammer blow'. The only way a reciprocating mass may be balanced is by opposing it with an equivalent reciprocating mass moving in the opposite direction. This had been grasped quite early in the development of the steam locomotive, as soon as the machines were capable of exceeding a walking pace. Many ingenious arrangements of cylinders were devised and tried, but the few that were simple enough to be viable were far ahead of the manufacturing techniques then available. Fortunately, it was discovered that by careful arrangement of segmental weights in the wheel rim, the worst effects of unbalanced reciprocating forces on the locomotive and train could be overcome, at the expense of greater effect on the permanent way.

As locomotive weights increased, the effect of hammer blow, the unbalanced vertical moment of the reciprocating pistons and their associated gear was becoming more and more important to the civil engineers, and they were looking askance at many projected designs. Although it took a long time for the principle to gain acceptance, it was appreciated that a well-designed multi-cylinder locomotive was kinder on the track and underline bridges.

Gresley took this a stage further by using high-tensile steel for the motion, the connecting and coupling rods and the valve gear. The mass of the motion could thereby be appreciably reduced, and hence its reciprocating imbalance was also greatly reduced. Naturally, the cost of the special steels was higher and the machining more expensive, and this point was frequently held against the Gresley designs. However, it was an initial cost, whereas the cost of replacing rails fractured by heavy hammer blow was a recurring cost, and to a lesser extent the reduced weight of the motion meant that

it took longer for the wheel bearings to develop a knock.

Three cylinders normally require three sets of valve gear. However, Harry Holcroft of the GWR had devised, in his spare time, an ingenious system of levers that allowed two sets of valve motion to drive three valves. It is important to grasp that his patent specification, produced in something of a hurry, did not completely cover the full application of his basic idea, and as a result Gresley was able to devise an arrangement that did not infringe the initial patent. To be fair, Gresley did offer Holcroft a job at Doncaster, but he was unable to take it up. One would like to think that the SECR offered him better terms, but from the guarded remarks in his biography, it seems more likely that he was held to his contract.

The conjugated valve gear was the weakest point in Gresley locomotive design, and it is difficult to see what actual savings accrued. There was more room on the crank-axle, but there was room in between the frames of a standard gauge locomotive to encompass not only two cranks,

Above: No 3686 as finished at Darlington Works in August 1943. It became LNER No 974 in 1946 and later BR No 60974.
Below: LNER class V.2 No 4844 *Coldstreamer*, as built at Doncaster, June 1939. Renumbered 873 in 1946 and later became 60873. It was withdrawn in 1964.
Left: Class V.2 No 4779, built at Darlington in September 1937. Later No 808 in 1946 and BR No 60808. Withdrawn in 1964.

but two eccentrics and still transmit all the power needed, without seriously weakening the main bearings, so this is not a valid argument. It is doubtful if the conjugated gear was any cheaper to make and install and in the case of most LNER locomotives some basic snags arose.

In general, the double rocker arms were placed in front of the cylinders, taking their drive from the far end of the two outside valve spindles. These spindles passed through the valve chest which, when the locomotive was running, was full of steam, some at boiler pressure and some at exhaust pressure. The valve spindles expanded as a result and this meant that the central valve settings differed when cold. This did not introduce any real uncertainty into the matter, for after the

Above: BR No 60833 at Darlington Shed in April 1961. Originally LNER class V.2 No 4804. It was built in 1938 and withdrawn in 1964.

Below: LNER No 3645 class V.2 as built at Darlington in 1942, in its wartime black livery. Withdrawn in 1964 as No 60943.

first half-dozen strokes the valves reached their working temperature. It was quite easy to make allowance for this when setting the valves, but it is said that Darlington did not do so. If this is so — and the story is a fairly persistent one that has never been refuted — then it is perhaps a comment on the relatively small effect of expansion, since there was no marked difference discernable in the overall performance of Darlington locomotives when compared with Doncaster machines. After all, the normal vertical movement of the axle-boxes within the frames could make quite appreciable differences to the valve settings.

The position of the gear in front of the cylinders had a more serious fault. Whenever it was necessary to remove any valve, or the centre piston, the rocker arms had to come down. This was the sort of additional job that fitters disliked, and was a serious fault in the arrangement. Conjugated gear had another snag, any alterations to the setting of the outer valves affected the inner one, and this made valve setting a long job. It had the advantage, however, that the valve gear was more accessible, and this eased loco-motive preparation. Many drivers liked it as a result, and this was undoubtedly a significant reason for its retention.

In practice the centre-valve 'over-ran' at speed, leading to the centre cylinder developing much more power. At first sight the effect seems improbable in the extreme, for the levers could hardly bend. However, Gresley's successor, Thompson, told O. S. Nock that the Darlington loco-motives went out new with additional clearance in the various bearings due to 'manu-facturing difficulties'! It is difficult to see what these could have been, for Darlington Works in North Eastern days was as well-equipped a factory as any in England and, at the onset of

World War II, Ministry of Supply inspectors were astounded by the precision standards normal in railway workshops.

Nevertheless, it was only on the LNER that conjugated valve gears were consistently applied to three-cylinder machines, and then only throughout Gresley's superintendency. There is no doubt that he had fixed ideas on the subject, but he also had a patent on the gear, and one of the recognised perquisites of high engineering rank is the exploita-tion of one's own inventions.

The conjugated gear worked well enough, though it did pro-duce some interesting sound effects which have been put forward as evidence of inefficient working. However, test results showed that once the initial use of short travel valves was replaced by the superior long travel valve, the Gresley locomotives could put up some excellent results.

Gresley not only maintained the larger pre-grouping classes side-by-side with the new engines, but where there seemed a reasonable probability that the improvements would show a financial benefit, he also recon-

structed certain classes to bring them more into line with modern ideas on cylinder design and valve events. Much of this make-do-and-mend policy was a result of financial restraint, which reduced the amount of money available for new construction, and did not permit the with-drawal or replacement of loco-motives which still had, in acturial terms, a large amount of working life left.

This particular aspect of his policy provided lineside observers with a pleasing variety of loco-motives. However, they were even more impressed by the Gresley machines, for they were invariably elegant. The boiler mountings looked right, but most important of all, the gentle reverse curves of the running board were probably the most pleasing solu-tion to the tricky business of marrying a high clearance over the driving wheels with the lower line set by the bufferbeam and cab. Gresley's locomotives fully lived up to the old design office dictum 'if it looks right, it is right'.
14

BR No 60911 at Leicester Central in July 1959. Originally it was LNER class V.2 No 4882.

Intermediate power

During the nineteenth century, it was the practice to employ down-rated express locomotives or free-running goods classes on the secondary passenger services and parcel trains. Neither arrangement was very satisfactory. By 1910, however, several of the older companies had begun to provide a special type of locomotive which was reasonably powerful but capable of a good turn of speed when required.

The type chosen was the 'Mogul' or 2-6-0, an arrangement that had long been in vogue in the USA, where it was derived from the 'American' type 4-4-0 with outside cylinders, substituting a smaller diameter six-coupled chassis with a leading two-wheeled truck under the same boiler and motion.

Although a few versions appeared towards the end of the nineteenth century, including some US imports on the Midland, it was not until early in the twentieth century that true Moguls appeared. On the GNR, Gresley introduced the K1 2-6-0 in 1912, the first design to appear after his appointment. This was a two-cylinder locomotive with 5 ft 8 in (1.72 m) diameter wheels, and proved a useful machine, and was succeeded in 1914 by a second series with a larger boiler.

These were successful machines, but Gresley was becoming more and more interested in three-cylinder drive, with conjugated valve gear, and in 1920 introduced the first of the K3 class of three-cylinder 2-6-0s. For their time, these were massive locomotives, with a 6 ft (1.83 m) diameter boiler barrel. The valves had a reasonably long travel, and the class multiplied to a total of 193 locomotives.

Taken in conjunction with the 75 two-cylinder 2-6-0s in the K2 class, and the normal supply of down-graded express locomotives that became available as more large locomotives were built, this class provided a good supply of modern mixed-traffic locomotives for the enlarged LNER.

The grouping of 1923 also had an important effect on locomotive workings over the Anglo-Scottish routes. In the old company days, in the case of the East Coast services, it had been normal practice to exchange locomotives at York. Although this was determined by company ownership, it was also extremely convenient for locomotive designers, since it had not been necessary to design a locomotive which could carry enough fuel for the full trip. The 1923 grouping put the entire run to Edinburgh under one administration, and there were obvious advantages in eliminating locomotive changes, on both the Kings Cross-Edinburgh trains and on the London-Newcastle services.

Fortunately the necessary locomotives were on hand. The North Eastern Railway had their Raven Pacifics, and the GNR the Gresley Pacifics. Trials were instituted and the Gresley design triumphed. How much this was due to the fact it was the CME's design is difficult to judge, but we can safely assume that over the North Eastern route there would be little enthusiasm to prove the potential of the 'foreign' locomotive. Although internecine rivalry never surfaced on the LNER as it did on the LMS, it certainly existed. No doubt the most significant factor in the selection of the Gresley design was that it fitted into the CME's grand strategy, whereas the Raven design was not really part of a concerted pattern.

The new company set about producing more and more Pacifics, initially the original low pressure version, later the improved high pressure machine, the A3 'Super Pacific'. The need was clear. The East Coast route now needed a large number of locomotives that could haul the principal trains to their furthest destinations without the need for engine interchange.

The LNER began operations with a pair of extremely good locomotives that met the immediate needs, and accordingly gave the design staff time to think seriously about the best form of secondary motive power. This was fortunate since the situation was changing.

In the 1920s road competition was being felt on an increasing scale as enterprising ex-servicemen sank their gratuities in a war surplus lorry and began a haulier's business. Many of these small operators did not survive for very long, but together they creamed off a significant proportion of the railway's most profitable traffic. At the same time, coach operators began to pose a real threat. The early charabanc, with its open seating and general air of unreliability had not been a serious competitor for regular middle-distance journeys. But as totally enclosed coaches with improved seating became available, the coach companies began to make inroads not only on local traffic, but also on the longer-distance journeys, where the real savings in terms of hard cash were much more significant. Of course, these services could not compete in terms of time, but to a very significant degree, they could compete on both convenience and comfort against the non-corridor train which, in the 1920s, was still quite common on secondary services.

The railways countered as best they could, largely by increasing the availability of corridor stock and the addition of restaurant or buffet facilities as new catering

cars became available. Naturally, the new stock was allocated to the principal expresses, and the stock so displaced moved down the scale. The East Coast route had long possessed some magnificent coaching stock, built whilst Gresley was in charge of carriage construction, but all this added materially to the dead weight hauled.

Two further Gresley designs of the late twenties, the D49 'Shire' or 'Hunt' class 4-4-0 of 1927 (total 76 locomotives) and the B17 'Sandringham' or 'Footballer' class 4-6-0 of 1928 (total 73 engines), produced a good batch of second line passenger locomotives for express services, but their 6 ft 8 in (2.03 m) diameter driving wheels, standard with the Pacifics, made them unsuitable for mixed-traffic duties.

The value of a large, mixed-

traffic locomotive had been dramatically demonstrated on the GWR when one of the 'Saint' class 4-6-0s had been fitted with 6 ft (1.83 m) diameter driving wheels to produce the prototype for the highly successful 'Hall' class. This type of locomotive was shown to have considerable value on fitted freight services, it was able to sustain fairly high speeds for long periods, and despite the slightly smaller wheel, was equally at home on fast passenger services. Such a locomotive was of inestimable value to both operating and running-shed staff. It was a good, reliable, go-anywhere, do-anything locomotive.

In the early 1930s, competition for parcels traffic became intense. Manufacturers required an overnight delivery, expecting goods despatched from their loading

Green Arrow BR No 60909 in September 1958 on a Newcastle down train near Potters Bar. It was built as LNER No 4880.

bank at the end of the working day to be waiting at their customer's the following morning. Road hauliers increasingly cut into this traffic, and it became of paramount importance that the railways could compete effectively by the use of fully-braked freight stock, scheduled to run at speeds around 60 mph (96 km/h) and more where suitable bogie and long wheelbase stock was available. More intermediate power locomotives were needed to do this, for the K3s tended to give a rough ride at speed, and to some extent were lacking in power. It was clear that a new mixed-traffic locomotive was required.

Stages in design

Some early locomotives, particularly from Brighton in the Craven regime, and from any of the North Eastern Works during Fletcher's benevolent reign, were designed in what seems today to have been a rather haphazard way, but by the turn of the century the process was more complicated and took considerably longer. In the gestation period many alternative designs were considered and frequently worked out in considerable detail, even to the point of estimating the probable weight of the finished machine.

Regrettably, records of many of the stages in the evolution of a design have been lost, but a number of locomotive engineers have realised recently that these abortive stages are of considerable interest, and have accordingly devoted a good deal of space in locomotive histories to a detailed consideration of the ones that got away.

For example, B. Spencer, in his extremely informative paper on the development of the LNER locomotive from 1923 to 1941 (given to the Institution of Locomotive Engineers on 19 March 1947), did not devote much space to the development of the V2 'Green Arrow' class 2-6-2, but he did raise a fascinating point. He revealed that prior to the development of the 2-6-2 design, Gresley had been considering a 2-6-4-4 arrangement with the tender articulated to the locomotive. Had it been built, it would have been one of the oddest-looking machines of all time, matched only by the booster-fitted versions of the NER Raven Atlantics. Yet Gresley was not an engineer who usually considered eccentric variations.

However, this proposal got well beyond the rough drawing stage; two locomotives were proposed and the classification K4 tentatively issued. The basic idea seems to have been to produce a version of the K3 more suited to high speeds.

In this instance, no booster was proposed for the articulating bogie, the general idea being to improve the rear control, and thus improve the riding qualities. At the same time, 6 ft 2 in (1.9 m) diameter driving wheels were substituted for the original 5 ft 8 in (1.7 m) wheels of the K3. The rest of the locomotive was to be more or less a standard K3, although the wheelbase was modified slightly to provide room for the articulating bogie.

The increase in driving wheel diameter meant that the boiler pitch had to be raised. The initial design, prepared at Darlington, had set it so high that there was virtually no room for boiler mountings, and although some ingenious ideas were put forward, it is unlikely that they would have proved very effective in service.

There were, however, other basic snags in the proposal. The cab had been lengthened to accommodate the rear mounting for the articulating bogie, and this would have led to complaints from the firemen. Equally, there almost certainly would have been a lot of caustic comments from shed foremen, since detaching the locomotives from the tender would have been a major operation, and would have presented difficulties when minor repairs had to be carried out on shed. We can be certain that there would have been very pointed comments on this feature.

A more serious fault arose under the firegate. To make room for the bogie, the trailing axle had been moved forward, and now sat more or less in the middle of the ashpan. Although there is no inherent problem in shielding the axle and the bearings from the heat of the grate, the necessary shroud would effectively divide the ashpan into two halves.

This particular arrangement had been tried on other locomotives, and almost without exception these machines were extremely erratic steamers, the few exceptions to this rule presenting enormous difficulties in this respect. The reason was partly that when clean, the passage of primary air was restricted in the middle of the grate, and the shroud soon received a build up of ash, effectively blocking the grate, leading to erratic combustion and all that this implies. The accepted cure of a stepped grate is little better, since it requires a rather more difficult firing technique which again leads to an indifferent performance.

Another, rather more practical, proposal was for a 4-6-0 with 6 ft 8 in (2.03 m) driving wheels and a narrow firebox version of a Pacific boiler. This too has been suggested as an alternative to the V2, but another interpretation is possible.

Gresley was not averse to considering the production of a relatively small class of locomotive, the P2s are an example. It is conceivable that the option was considered of building a moderate number of fairly fast freight locomotives, similar in purpose to the GWR large-boilered 4700 2-8-0s, together with another class of powerful 4-6-0s to work turn and turn about with Pacifics on the major services. Some extra costs would have been involved, but it is more sensible to tailor a locomotive to a precise duty, rather than produce large numbers of a compromise locomotive which, whilst capable of performing any duty competently, would not do anything well. Such a policy is extremely attractive to a design office, and there are indications that this option was still open when the first V2s entered service.

Above: V.2 No 60926 at Prestonpans with an up freight. The black BR livery with original tender totem is clearly visible.

Below: The vintage Rolls parked on the lane adds a pleasing touch to the setting as V.2 No 60919 passes near Cove Bay in March 1959. This is a typical arrangement adopted by modellers to mask a scenic break.

Above: Immaculate in BR black, No 60800 *Green Arrow* stands waiting to leave Doncaster shed in March 1954.

Below: No 60809 *The Snapper* passing Markham with a lightly-loaded down express in May 1961.

Above: V.2 No 60848 on an up relief, with carmine and cream stock, passes through Barkston Junction in May 1959.

Below: In BR lined black, with original tender totem, V.2 No 60872 *King's Own Yorkshire Light Infantry* is seen at its appropriate home shed in York – September 1959.

Above: In immaculate condition, 60884 is seen here at the head of the up postal near Cove Bay in March 1959.

Below: On the work for which it was designed, V.2 No 60903 in BR green livery heads a fitted freight on Gamston curve.

Above: Leaving the Tay Bridge at Wormit in October 1965, V.2 No 60836 heads an up freight. Note the large steam pipes fitted when the original monobloc cylinders were replaced with three separate units.

Below: *Green Arrow* on display at Barnet in 1937, as built.

V.2 No 60836 leaves Dundee for Perth in August 1966 with an UP Freight.

Above: No 60964, *The Durham Light Infantry* at Haymarket shed in 1957.

Below: V.2 No 60817, fitted with double chimney, passes through Hitchin with an up express in 1962.

Above: V.2 No 60941 passing Amersham
with the 12:38 Marylebone-Nottingham
express.. London transport 'A' stock stands
on the up line.

Below: Preserved and restored to its original
appearance, No 4771 *Green Arrow* heads the
special restaurant car train near Hessay in
September 1979.

Green Arrows in detail

In selecting a 2-6-2 arrangement for the new locomotive, Gresley broke with established practice for a British mixed-traffic locomotive. There can be little doubt that his main object here was to use a wide firebox boiler, and with the benefit of hindsight this idea can be seen to have had considerable merit. However, it is highly unlikely that he could have suspected that well before the normal lifespan of his locomotives had been reached, the quality of locomotive coal would have deteriorated to the point where there would be a distinct advantage in a wide grate. The suggestion that Yorkshire coal made this arrangement preferable is somewhat wide of the mark; the grade normally used by the LNER at the time was completely acceptable for the narrow fireboxes fitted to several Gresley designs.

The boiler was very similar to the one fitted to the A3 Pacifics, but two feet shorter in the barrel. The exact difference is 1 ft 11 in (0.61 m) but although Doncaster was working to precise limits, it is doubtful if they were able to produce a riveted boiler barrel to that degree of precision. From the outset the V2 boilers were fitted with the elongated rear projection to the dome that housed the new pattern steam collector, and had first been seen on the P2 class 2-8-2s.

The idea behind this arrangement was to increase the area over which steam was drawn, in order to prevent undue frothing of the water in the boiler. It was analogous to the GWR system of a perforated pipe over the firebox, but was external to the boiler shell. It also served to increase the steam space around the regulator, for although the old term persisted for the fitting, the steady increase in boiler diameters from 1900 onwards had changed the dome from a large, well-rounded object to an overgrown manhole cover, which was hidden by an extremely squashed casing. On larger British locomotives, the dome was more a raised cover to the regulator than anything else. Gresley's 'banjo dome' was a simple and reasonably effective device which appeared to do its work well.

The shorter barrel, together with the inevitable shorter tubes, seemed in practice to have improved the steaming qualities of the boiler, since there is no evidence that the Green Arrows were ever lacking in this direction. The superheating elements were increased in size over the Pacifics, giving the class an even higher degree of superheat than usual in most Gresley designs.

The driving wheels were 6 ft 2 in (1.88 m) in diameter, identical to the P2 class 2-8-2s, and were arranged over a very long coupled wheelbase of 7 ft 3 in (2.2 m) and 8 ft 3 in (2.5 m), exceeded only in Britain by the GWR 'King' class. This almost certainly resulted from the boiler design, and the wheels were clearly laid out to look pleasing beneath the selected boiler. Other features of this model included a standard rear axle arrangement, with outside axleboxes arranged to slide laterally on the Cartazzi principle; the leading pony truck had its side movement controlled by swing links, in common with other Gresley designs. The plate frames were 1 in (25 mm) thick, and in practice appeared trouble-free.

As with the P2s, the cylinders formed a monobloc casting, and included the steampipes to the outside cylinders. Monobloc castings were not new, they had been used on the NER in Raven's day, but these incorporated vastly improved internal passages based on the principles laid down by Chapelon, who developed the practice of 'internal streamlining' with his famous compound locomotives.

The principle takes into account that the ease with which the steam can flow around the system is of vital importance at high power outputs. Of course, steam can take quite tortuous paths, as it must when passing through a superheater, but here the total cross section is quite large, and the restriction on the flow is acceptable. A different set of conditions around the cylinders and the shape of the passages has been shown to have a critical effect on the working of an engine at speed.

In addition to the design, the actual manufacture of a set of monobloc cylinders poses considerable technical problems. For example, the patterns are extremely complex and numerous cores have to be made. When the main mould has been prepared, these have to be placed precisely in position in the holes provided.

The production of a sand mould for a monobloc cylinder set is the pinnacle of the foundryman's craft, matched only by the skill needed to ensure a complete pour to attain a perfect casting. Compared with all this, the machining of the cylinder block is relatively straightforward. Although the centre cylinder was set at a different angle to the outer pair, and they were all angled relative to the vertical plane, such complications were easily dealt with by the use of extremely sophisticated machine tools.

Whether there was any real advantage in this technique is a moot point. There was no gain in strength, for a central cylinder casting would have provided an excellent cross member on its own. Although three separate castings would have involved slightly more machining, and a little more work in the erection bay, the castings would have been simplified and the risk of a single expensive item being ruined at any stage in manufacture would have been eliminated. It is significant that, when cylinder blocks need replacement towards the end of the locomotives' lives, the monobloc was abandoned in favour of three entirely new separate castings.

One virtue of the in-line arrangement was that all connecting rods were of identical length although not of identical design, since the centre big end had to have split bearings. The outside connecting rods were somewhat shorter than was customary in Gresley practice, though not in any way exceptional in this respect.

The three cylinders drove the centre axle and, to compensate for the different angle of the centre engine necessary to allow the motion to clear the leading axle, the centre crank was 9° off the true 120° location. This small displacement was supposed to have deleterious effects on the performance, but in view of the class's subsequent record there seems to be little evidence of this. It was a consequence of the conjugated drive, and the arrangement is a perfectly acceptable aspect of design compromise.

The conjugated drive to the centre valve was mounted in front of the cylinders, and this arrangement was criticised on two grounds. Firstly because the centre valve events are affected by the expansion of the outside valve spindles; secondly, the gear restricted access to the centre cylinder and to all valves, and had to be dismantled in order that any maintenance to these parts could be carried out.

Although the majority of the class had normal regulators in the dome, Nos 4804 and 4806, 'The

Green Howard', were fitted with MLS multiple-valve regulators in the smokebox, operated by external rodding, similar to that subsequently fitted to the BR standard classes. This equipment was later removed, although MLS valves were used on the Peppercorn A2s. The regulator fitted to the V2s was of the normal Gresley pattern with pull-out regulator handle; but on this class it tended to allow enough steam to leak through in the 'closed' position to make the locomotive move of its own accord. To counter this, the drain cocks were left open, but not surprisingly this fault was sufficient to make the class extremely unpopular when it moved to other regions after nationalisation. The Western even contemplated banning the class completely! A modified regulator, similar to the NER pattern, allowed more sensitive handling.

The cab fittings followed standard Gresley practice and were substantially similar to those on the Pacifics, a fact that undoubtedly endeared the class to enginemen used to turn-and-turn-about with the larger machines. The V-fronted cab introduced with the P2s was adopted because it was claimed that by angling the spectacle glass in this fashion there was less chance of glare.

The running board was carried clear of the driving wheels, eliminating the vestigial splashers that most British steam locomotives still acquired. This was a practical arrangement, since the provision of mechanical lubrication and other refinements had also eliminated the need for an engineman to get out in front during the journey to attend to some part that was running dry. The provision of full-width cabs had made this practice even more hazardous than before, and so the running board was only needed for convenience on shed — and here, the higher it was the better.

From the turn of the century, when multi-level running boards had come into use, the problem of linking them in an agreeable fashion had vexed designers. At the outset Churchward had not even attempted to do this, introducing an uncompromising and eminently practical vertical division. Gresley's solution, two elegant reverse curves, was easily the best visual solution, and had one very desirable feature, the locomotives looked like flyers.

The majority of the class received the later pattern six wheeled tender, holding 7½ tons (7620 kg) of coal and 4,200 gallons (19,093 litres) of water. A few of the class received the earlier pattern, with stepped-out coal rails. As usual, tenders were interchanged over the years as the locomotives came in for overhauls.

Visually there was very little change in the locomotives throughout their lives. In 1947 No 813 (later numbering) received a stovepipe chimney with small deflector plates and, as will be discussed later, several of the older locomotives were fitted with multiple blastpipes.

Initially, it was announced that the locomotives would be turned out in the black livery reserved for freight locomotives, an indication that their original role was restricted. However, they were outshopped in full passenger livery. A few years later, wartime austerity decreed an all-black finish with NE on the tender, and under BR they originally appeared in the quasi-LNWR lined black livery. Later, in common with other mixed-traffic classes mainly employed on passenger duties, they were painted in the GWR style green. By that time locomotive cleaning had become virtually impossible on British Railways, the ready supply of young men prepared to spend a couple of years at this thankless task in order to gain promotion to the footplate having

Above: LNER 2–6–2 class V.2 No 4806, *The Green Howards*, as built at Darlington in 1938. Later it became No 835 and BR No 60835, and was withdrawn in 1946. Class V.2 in early British numbering and lettering before the adoption of the 'Hungry Lion' crest. No 60834 was originally built at Darlington as LNER No 4805.

Right: BR No 60946 in store at Thornaby Shed in June 1963, next to a withdrawn Austerity class freight locomotive.

virtually disappeared.

However, this was in the future, and the new locomotives were well received by enthusiasts. They looked like thoroughbreds and they were elegant and graceful compared with the near-contemporary LMS Black fives. At this point it is worth comparing the three main mixed-traffic classes of the period in tabular fashion:

It will be seen that the main difference was the relatively high axle load of the V2, this was one of the side advantages of the

better balanced three-cylinder drive. The total length of the wheelbase had one small disadvantage, it meant that the locomotives could not be turned on a 55 ft (16.76 m) table, and therefore they could not undertake certain duties formerly carried out by K3 locomotives unless the facilities at the outer termini were modernised. It seems clear that when the class was under design this possibility had been firmly ruled out in the immediate future.

Although the class began with the proposition that a more

BR No 60882 in September 1962 approaching Perth Station. Originally it was LNER class V.2 No 4853.

powerful version of the K3 was required, it is fairly certain that quite early in the gestation it was appreciated that, with its extremely large boiler, the K3 was just about as large and powerful a machine as could be built within that particular length. The V2s have often been described as cut-down Pacifics, but with several details in common with the P2s, they are really a smaller version of that class.

Mixed Traffic Locomotives of Great Britain, 1924–1936

	GWR 49XX	LMS 5P5F	LNER V2
Wheel arrangement	4-6-0	4-6-0	2-6-2
Date introduced	1924*	1934	1936
Driving wheel diameter	6 ft 0 in (1.8 m)	6 ft 0 in (1.8 m)	6 ft 2 in (1.88 m)
Coupled wheelbase	7 ft (2.1 m) and 7 ft 9 in (2.36 m)	7 ft (2.1 m) and 8 ft (2.4 m)	7 ft 3 in (2.2 m) and 8 ft 3 in (2.5 m)
Total wheelbase	53 ft 4½ in (16.2 m)	52 ft 2¾ in (15.8 m)	56 ft 2⅛ in (17.1 m)
Overall length	63 ft 0¼ in (19.2 m)	63 ft 7¾ in (19.4 m)	66 ft 5⅛ in (20.24 m)
Maximum axle load	18 tons 19 cwt (19,254 kg)	17 tons 18 cwt (18,187 kg)	22 tons (22,353 kg)
Cylinders	two	two	three
Cylinders: bore × stroke	18½ in (48 cm) × 30 in (76.2 cm)	18½ in (48 cm) × 28 in (71.12 cm)	18½ in (48 cm) × 26 in (66 cm)
Boiler pressure psi	225	225	220
Nominal tractive effort	27,275 lb (12,372 kg)	25,455 lb (11,546 kg)	27,420 lb (12,438 kg)

* Prototype conversion of 'Saint'. The main construction began in 1928.

Green Arrows in service

Only five of the new V2 class were built at Doncaster at first, and these were sent to various sheds around the system for evaluation. This was almost a formality since the majority of enginemen took to them at once. Although from the observer's point of view the locomotive had a number of novel features, as far as the crew were concerned it was a familiar machine that worked in the way they preferred.

The proposals were that the new locomotives would generally be confined to fast fitted freights, and would only work passenger duties in the event of trouble, or to balance a locomotive diagram. But it was soon discovered that, despite their smaller driving wheels and shorter boiler, in day-to-day working they were every bit as good as the A3 Pacifics, and were rostered accordingly.

Details survive of a run of No 4771 on the 10.53 relief to Newcastle and Sunderland, on this occasion loaded to 600 tons (609,638 kg). It was expected that with its smaller wheels the driver would run rather faster uphill than was usual with the Pacifics; this belief was fostered by the fact that the first P2, No 2001 (*Cock o' the North*) had been worked in this fashion during its trials. However, this was a normal service train and the driver proceeded to work the train in the conventional manner, taking the up-grades steadily and then, once over the summit, opening up and running freely downhill.

Although less spectacular than many observers would like, this method of driving is generally more economical. Leaving aside any question of saving coal which, in the absence of a generous bonus to drivers, is largely academic, there is the point that it eases the work of the fireman, and when two men have to work together as a crew consideration for one's mate makes for better all-round performance.

What is most significant about this is that it is a clear indication that even with a heavy load the V2s were fully masters of their work, having enough reserves in hand to allow them to tackle out-of-the-way slacks, or even, in emergency, to tackle something well outside their theoretical capacity. Such an occasion occurred when a V2 had to take over for a failed A4 on the 'West Riding Limited'.

Regrettably, no recorder was on the train to provide details of the run, but it was exceptional by any standards. The inevitable delay in exchanging engines meant that not only did it make a late start from Kings Cross but, out of its proper path, it was subject to some signal delays. The locomotive only dropped some four minutes on a tightly-timed schedule, despite the many disadvantages. This was one of the most sprightly pieces of work by any British mixed-traffic locomotive at that time.

The V2s were shown to be more than ready to rise to the occasion when called upon, and not only were they substituted for A4s in emergencies, but by the summer of 1939 were also being rostered to work the 'Yorkshire Pullman', turn and turn about with Pacifics. Although this was not one of the LNER's major services it was a prestige train, normally loading about nine Pullman cars of the old, heavy-weight pattern. Much as this type of vehicle is loved by the percipient train traveller, it is an extremely inconvenient vehicle from the operator's point of view.

To the afficionado the modern versions with plastic interiors and normal coach bodies, were not the same, even when painted in the correct colours, and support dwindled as a result. But in the pre-war days a Pullman train was the genuine article, and the users were more knowledgeable, and more voluble travellers.

Certainly, the V2s were proving to be superb locomotives, and although still rated as mixed-traffic machines, it is clear that the operating staff were treating them as powerful passenger locomotives with the side advantage that they could tackle fast fitted freight into the bargain. This was virtually a complete turnabout from the original concept. They were increased in numbers, 20 appearing in 1937, 19 in 1938 and 42 in 1939, making the total 86, with more under construction. All question of the high-powered 4-6-0 seems to have ended.

The axle load of 22 tons limited the spread of the class to the major routes, but there was ample work for them to do. In the case of the Great Central division, their arrival was delayed, for until the turntables were replaced in 1938, both the V2s and Pacifics were prevented from working over these lines. Only a few V2s were transferred to this division, even by 1947 Gorton only had four. On the Great Central it appears that the class was seen as the equivalent of the Pacifics, and they worked the major services indiscriminately. At first there were some complaints that they rolled on the descent from Woodhead, but clearly this was not taken seriously at the time, although it led to comment some 15 years later.

The pre-war experience was wholly favourable. The class was able to show its worth on the fast fitted freights, for which it was presumably intended. Its ability to run fast with heavy loads possibly came as a pleasant

V.2 No 60910 in September 1962

surprise to all concerned. 'Green Arrows' were also found on passenger duties as a matter of course; they effectively displaced the GNR Atlantics from relief duties, much to the relief of the shed staff. Having a powerful modern locomotive with convenient, comfortable cabs was pleasure enough in itself, and to be able to relegate the rough-riding Atlantics to secondary duties doubtlessly was regarded as an extremely useful bonus. Whatever its attractions may be to the lineside observer, a class that is apt to travel nearly as far sideways as it does forward, is not liked by drivers or firemen.

There is no doubt that in the V2 the LNER had a locomotive that might well have helped thwart road competition during the early 1940s. After a long period of resigned acceptance, the railway companies were beginning to attack the opposition. The 'Fair Deal' campaign of 1938, publicised under a prophetic 'British Railways' heading, tried to influence public opinion towards amendments in the law governing freight rates and conditions. The companies believed, with some justification, that these rates and conditions were weighted against them, having been formulated in the days

when they held a virtual monopoly of inland transport. Whether this campaign would have had any lasting effect is hard to say. Parliament has never been quick off the mark in such matters, and is apt to leave things as they are in the hope that the problem will go away, except where some matter of party principle is involved. In any case, Parliament had more pressing worries, and these came to a head in August 1939. War was declared on Germany on 3 September, and the railways came under Government control for the second time in this century.

Little sisters

Although the production of the V2 had provided the LNER with an extremely useful machine, it had not solved the problem of the K3 2-6-0. Useful as these machines were, they were fitted with relatively small driving wheels, and were also somewhat lively at speed. There was still a need for an improved design that could work over the lighter routes of the company.

Just as the V2s could be regarded as a smaller version of the P2s, the V4 2-6-2 was an even smaller machine with the same pedigree. With the new design, the Gresley tendencies towards high-class design and construction were possibly taken a little too far, considering the intended purpose of the loco-motive. It was fitted with 5 ft 8 in (1.73 m) drivers, and three cylin-ders were arranged in line, a sound design since the thrust of the outside cylinders was not on to an unsupported frame and, as with the V2s, connecting rods were of the same length, and the conjugated valve gear was placed in front. The cylinders were fairly small, 15 in (38 cm) diameter, 26 in (66 cm) stroke.

The boiler, too, was small, only 5 ft 4 in (1.62 cm) diameter tapering to 4 ft 8 in (1.4 m) but was pressed to 250 psi. It was also made from 2 per cent nickel steel and the second and last of the class also had a thermic syphon in the firebox. A short tender was attached carrying six tons (6,096 kg) of coal and 3,500 gallon (15,911 litre) water tanks. Wartime problems meant that construction of the initial pair was protracted, and they did not appear until 1941, the first, No 3401 'Bantam Cock' appear-ing only six weeks before Gresley's death. Further construc-tion ceased, the new CME having

totally different ideas on the subject of mixed traffic engines. The two locomotives endured a rather lonely career.

There is no doubt whatsoever that they were superb machines. With the benefit of hindsight it has been suggested they were much too good for the job they were built to perform, to haul important trains over secondary routes. However, they were con-ceived before the railways went into decline, and like the V2s were originally intended to spear-head a revival. With a light axle

load, just 17 tons (17,273 kg), and three-cylinder drive, they were kind on the track. The 2-6-2 arrangement is also to be pre-ferred on lightly-built lines for whether travelling forward or tender first, the rigid wheelbase is eased into any curves and there is less tendency to spread the gauge. The wide firebox not only made them happy with relatively poor coal, it eased the fireman's work appreciably, since the small grate was a good deal shorter as a result. The rear idle axle, carried in Cartazzi boxes, improved the riding, and as they were not called upon to perform prodigies of haulage they were delightfully smooth-running machines.

No doubt, had the class multi-

Light 2-6-2 Class V4	LNER
Wheel arrangement	2-6-2
Date introduced	1941
Driving wheel diameter	5 ft 8 in (1.72 m)
Coupled wheelbase	6 ft 6 in (1.98 m) and 6 ft 4 in (1.93 m)
Total wheelbase	50 ft 2¼ in (15.24 m)
Overall length	59 ft 9 in (18.21 m)
Maximum axle load	17 tons (17,273 kg)
Cylinders	three
Cylinders: bore × stroke	15 in × 26 in (38 × 66 cm)
Boiler pressure psi	250
Nominal tractive effort	27,420 lb (12,438 kg)

plied, sundry changes might have taken place. The thermic syphon was removed because it proved much more trouble than it was worth under the normal usage of locomotives. No 3402 had to lie idle whilst the alterations took place, since there were no spare boilers provided; with only two locomotives, this would have been wasteful. If more had been built, it is possible that a V4/2 class with 220 psi boilers and larger bore cylinders could have been produced, for the very special nature of the boiler undoubtedly increased the first cost.

The class is supposed to have been expensive to maintain, but this has always been the lot of small classes or single locomotives. Moreover, the three-cylinder design was much kinder on the track than the two-cylinder machines that superseded them, and it is probable that, overall, there would have been very little in it.

The importance of the V4 in the Gresley strategy can only be properly understood in relation to the V2. In the latter, the LNER had a locomotive tailored for general purpose express duties on the main line. The V4 was to provide the same sort of service on cross country routes. In the event, the two representatives spent their days in Scotland, but it could be argued that they would have been far more use in East Anglia. If we think of them as replacing the aging 4-4-0s on secondary services, it is possible to see that, but for the war, the V4 could have halted the drift away from rail travel on secondary routes by providing a brighter, faster and generally more acceptable service.

As it was, the grand strategy was thwarted by events in Europe. Nos 3401 'Bantam Cock' and 3402, unnamed, but unofficially known as 'Bantam Hen', proved to be the last flourish of the Gresley era.

Wartime duties

The 'Green Arrows' were conceived, not as a conventional mixed-traffic locomotive, but as a fast freight and secondary express engine. What is not fully appreciated perhaps, was that the LNER clearly was getting away from the concept of slow, plodding goods trains and moving into an era where only a limited amount of freight would travel in this fashion. Meanwhile, the bulk of the profitable merchandise was moved quickly, expeditiously, and safely over reserved tracks, and where possible from factory siding to warehouse loading bank. With the fast freights travelling at speeds hitherto reserved for passengers, the freight customer would be delighted and they would fit into the timetables alongside passenger trains, to their mutual advantage.

This magnificent concept disappeared overnight on the declaration of war, but the V2s, which had already proved to be more versatile than anyone could have hoped, demonstrated that their potential was far from exhausted. But first, an important by-product of their classification came into play.

At the outbreak of war, the railways came under government control, and the dead hand of officialdom descended on the lines. In short, strict controls were introduced without even bothering to see if these were absolutely necessary. One such fiat was that no more express passenger locomotives could be built. The V2s were of course mixed-traffic, and it could be shown that they had been intended for freight work; of course, in wartime freight was very important. It was irrelevant that passenger demand had increased as a result of military call-up and evacuation and the

subsequent spreading of families about the country; private travel was frivolous in the extreme, and had to be made uncomfortable.

However, it was perfectly all right to build mixed-traffic locomotives, and so more V2s were laid down. No less than 98 were built between 1940 and 1942, over half the class, making a total of 184, then production was stopped prematurely. Furthermore, as the strain on the railway system grew, the value of this extremely versatile class of locomotive became even more apparent.

The fast fitted freights were, of course, no more. The high speed expresses were also done away with and fairly low overall speeds were the order, not of the day, but of the Ministry. The speed potential of the 'Green Arrows' and of other Gresley locomotives was no longer so important. The haulage power of the V2s was about to be tested.

Records of wartime running are scarce, for the generally overcrowded nature of trains, especially at weekends, made it difficult for an observer to get a vantage point where he could see the vital timing points. There was not much point standing in the corridor or in the vestibule, since these were usually filled with service personnel and their kitbags. However, the overall performance was easily judged, for trains of phenomenal length were easily noted, and on the East Coast route long trains soon became commonplace.

One of the heaviest trains ever hauled on British metals, was

V.2 No 60910 in an unkempt condition on Carlisle to Edinburgh freight duty and BR No 60801 in September 1962, passing Hilton Junction Box.

headed by a V2, No 4800, which took a 26 coach load, 746 tons (757,984 kg) tare, 860 tons (873,815 kg) or more gross, from Peterborough to Kings Cross in a matter of 102 minutes, not exactly fast for the 76½ mile (123 km) journey, but an extremely creditable performance with a train almost twice the size for which the class was designed. Although, in terms of sheer hard work it is unlikely that any other V2 did better, in terms of sheer deadweight, a rather more interesting performance was put up by No 4886 on a run from Newcastle to Grantham.

The load in this instance was a mere 20 coaches, or about 700 tons (711,245 kg). The train took 95 minutes to cover the 80¼ miles (129 km) from Newcastle to York, then proceeded to run the rest of the journey to Grantham, some 83 miles (133.5 km), in 98 minutes. Speeds of 60 mph (96.5 km/h) were regularly attained and some 11½ minutes was gained on the wartime schedule. Unfortunately, as with so many locomotive performance logs, the records completely ignore what is perhaps the most important factor of all, and there is no indication as to whether the train actually kept time. It is unlikely that it did under wartime conditions.

One reason for this was extended station times, caused by a number of different factors. For example, there were fewer porters, and as the war drew on women replaced the men. Whatever feminists may claim, it can be argued that a woman is not as strong as a man, and where parcels and mailbags have to be taken out of an overcrowded van, the man has a distinct advantage. There were also generally far more parcels to unload than in peace time, perhaps a more important point. Trains were crowded, and there were plenty of people anxious to get on. All this took longer, particularly as a high proportion of travellers were servicemen on a posting, burdened

V.2 class No 60885, formerly LNER No 4856, on a Saltburn to Glasgow express passing Monkton Hall Junction in July 1962.

with kitbags. The traditional British carriage door was not designed for easy egress, it harked back to a golden age when passengers left their luggage to be loaded into the van by waiting minions who did the donkey work whilst their lords and ladies travelled in style.

Most important of all was the East Coast predilection for over-long trains. These frequently ran late, not because they were beyond the capacity of the loco-motives — on the easier wartime schedules a V2 or a Pacific could tackle such loads. The reason was rather more obvious, they were too long for the platforms. At intermediate stations this frequently meant that the train had to be drawn up a second time, which effectively tripled station time. But the problems which arose at Kings Cross were of quite a different kind when, with the Pacific or V2 hard against the buffers by the con-course, the tail was stretching across all the approach roads and well on its way into Gas Works Tunnel, bringing the terminus to a halt. The train had to be split, and the second half shunted into another platform. This could be quite a problem if the last coach fouled the outer pointwork.

Before long, commonsense took over, and trains were restricted to around 18 coaches, still over-long for the platforms, but manageable. It was possible to avoid a double draw-up on such a train; the rear coaches were marked 'Kings Cross Only', and passengers for intermediate stops were persuaded to get along the corridors well in advance — or risk getting carried past their destination.

Not all wartime runs showed great enterprise on the part of the crews. They had a difficult job because maintenance standards were being allowed to decline. It cannot be over-emphasised that much of the underlying strength of the Gresley tradition lay in the quality of craftsmanship, not merely in the main works, but

in the running sheds. Many of the design features were adopted because it was known that the locomotives would get careful attention from the fitters in the sheds.

As the war drew on, conditions deteriorated. Many sheds were badly damaged during air raids and although the maintenance bays were patched up the conditions under which the men had to work were very difficult. On top of this, virtually every component was in short supply, and although as an essential industry railways had a degree of priority, there were still not enough to go round. Frequently a locomotive had to be patched up and put back into service, when in happier times it would have had parts replaced with new or completely overhauled components sent direct from the works.

The locomotive crews themselves were enduring harsh conditions. They were working long hours and footplate conditions were poor. For example, there was the question of the black-out, which meant that tarpaulins were rigged from cab to tender. At times this could produce a very snug arrangement; at others it was stifling. The coal was of poor quality and above all, with fewer men on shed, the overall condition of the machines deteriorated. It can be argued that, except as a matter of pride, it makes little difference to a driver if the boiler is sparkling clean or utterly filthy, but all too often the filth found its way into the cab as well. This was partly due to the introduction of common user turns, but the root of the problem was a sheer lack of manpower.

The most important factor was wartime rationing. Anyone undertaking hard manual labour on a civilian wartime diet was perpetually hungry. Firemen, traditionally a wiry group, were hard hit, since shovelling several tons of coal across a moving footplate day in and day out burns up the calories; many became gaunt and all were weary. Often, a lack-lustre performance on the part of a locomotive was the result of an over-tired, underfed fireman being unable to rise to the occasion. The men did at times pull something out of the hat. For example, there is the case of driver Skerritt of Grantham, who took over an express in an emergency and, with No 4851, kept to sectional time between Retford and Grantham. This was creditable under any circumstances; what made this particular run eventful was that he did it running tender first!

Such devotion to duty was unusual, but by no means unique. Driver Skerritt's achievement stands for the unsung efforts of the great majority of railwaymen during wartime. As for the V2s themselves, it has often been said that they were the 'engines that won the war'. Like all such claims, it is a hyperbole, but although other claims have been put forward, no one would seriously refute the statement that under wartime conditions, the 184 2-6-2s performed prodigious amounts of work under conditions their designers hardly envisaged.

BR class V.2 No 60894 (formerly LNER No 4865) at Darlington Shed in April 1961 surrounded by Austerity class freight locomotives.

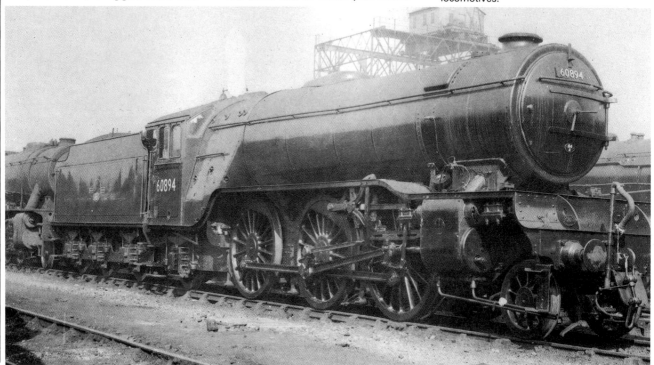

Thompson's reforms

In the latter years of the war, the V2s faced a particular problem that exacerbated the existing difficulties facing all locomotives. It arose from a tragic event. On 5 April 1941, Sir Nigel Gresley died suddenly and was succeeded by Edward Thompson, son-in-law of Sir Vincent Raven and a North Eastern man at heart. He had little time for many of Gresley's practices, and in particular he was opposed to the conjugated valve gear.

O. S. Nock has put on record that Thompson said that the Doncaster Works — where most of the V2s were built — had been in the habit of turning out loco-motives with ample clearance in all the valve gear bearings and pins. The movement of the centre valve was somewhat erratic, as a result when the locomotive was travelling at speed, higher stresses were imposed on the centre big end, thus exacerbating the problems of lubrication.

It must be appreciated however, that the reciprocating steam engine with slide or piston valves is an extremely tolerant machine, and that although the exact setting of the valve events can make quite an appreciable difference to the indicator cards, in day-to-day working, the effects are minimal. There is no question that every senior man at Darlington understood this. The theoretical efficiency may be impaired but the difference, expressed as a percentage, is very small indeed. A far greater variation will be experienced as a result of driving techniques. For example, a driver who goes up a bank in fine style, blasting a high proportion of the fire out of the chimney, will produce some spectacular effects and may well gladden the heart of an enthusiast, but all the unburnt and partially burned fuel spread around the countryside materially reduces the thermal efficiency of the cycle.

The truth is that the locomo-tives which, according to rumour, were leaving Doncaster Works with their valve gear slack and the centre valve incorrectly set were the very machines that put up so many creditable perform-ances between 1937 and 1941. It is possible that their perform-ance could have been improved had the various parts been put precisely on their theoretical settings. But the fact remains that the main result of an apparent degree of laxity at Doncaster was that all Gresley three-cylindered locomotives had a tendency to produce some very interesting sound effects — the syncopated Gresley beat. This was used by the running foreman as a very effective means of telling when a locomotive was due for an intermediate overhaul.

The more serious implication is that there was bitter enmity between Thompson and Gresley. Thousands of words have been written on the subject, mostly by Gresley supporters, with a little by those who favoured Thompson. As a result, a good deal of mud has been stirred up and the real culprit has been allowed to get away with what can best be described as an incredibly inept piece of management.

There is no suggestion what-soever that Thompson was antagonistic towards his chief, and plenty of evidence that he was a loyal, conscientious servant of the LNER. Had he shown any sign of disloyalty, he would not have been promoted. The fact he was son-in-law of Sir Vincent Raven and a man who, but for the grouping, would have been in the running for a high position on the North Eastern Railway, is totally irrelevant in the world in which the LNER was formed in 1923. He was a capable engineer, a sound administrator, and had some extremely good ideas on locomotive design, which just happened to run counter to everything Gresley favoured.

Although he was irascible, he was not the only CME to have a fiery temper, or to exhibit signs of authoritarian behaviour. When one looks at the duties and responsi-bilities of a Chief Mechanical Engineer of any large railway —

Just visiting. BR No 60916 from Darlington at Thornaby Shed in June 1963.

which extend far beyond the extremely pleasant business of preparing the design of new locomotives — it is surprising that so few gave vent to their feelings from time to time. When, on one memorable occasion, he threw a weight through a double-glazed window, it was because a strict order, laid down for his own personal well-being, had been disobeyed. Any nineteenth century locomotive superintendent would have marked the occasion by dismissing the offender on the spot, but in the 1940s, this option was denied to Thompson, who only did what most of us would dearly love to do under similar circumstances.

The man responsible for the apparent feud was without doubt Sir Ronald Matthews, chairman of the LNER. Thompson was appointed CME at the fairly advanced age of 60, in the early years of what he must have known would be a protracted war. He was then told by the Chairman that there was no need for him to consider any new locomotives, the Gresley designs

were excellent and could be continued.

This must have come as a great shock, for, whatever one may say about the Gresley designs, it is clear that they called for a level of expertise and maintenance that was unlikely to return in the fore-seeable future. In all probability Thompson, as a sound, practical engineer came prepared with proposals for a range of utilitarian machines to carry the LNER through a period where the finesse of Gresley's machines could not come into play. Not surprisingly he offered his resig-nation, not outright, but should an independent referee find against his conclusions concern-ing Gresley's designs in general and the conjugated valve gear in particular. It was the action of a reasonable man; a thoughtless comment by the Chairman pushed Thompson into a position no other CME ever faced — he had to prove his predecessor's work at fault.

The invidious position as referee fell to Sir William Stanier, who was the only locomotive

Above: *Green Arrow*, BR No 60800, emerging from Hadley Wood tunnel.
Right: *Green Arrow* restored with No 4472 *Flying Scotsman* at Steamtown Museum, Carnforth.

engineer of suitable stature available. His report was guarded, but of the valve gear, he simply said that he would not use it himself — and having designed several three-cylinder locomotives and rebuilt another class, he was presumably speaking from the heart. And in fact, it was only on the LNER under Gresley that three-cylinder conjugated valve gear was used with any great degree of enthusiasm. Elsewhere it was tried and quietly abandoned.

Thompson gained his point. He was not able to alter the locomotives already built, but he did stop the construction of the last four V2s scheduled, and from them produced a small class of Pacifics, the A2/1s.

One of the most popular pastimes among locomotive students is to speculate on what might have happened had the design been slightly different. In the case of the 'Green Arrows' the temptation is overwhelming, for the use of a shortened A3 boiler and a very extended wheelbase, plus the preference that exists in many quarters for a leading two-wheel truck, leads one to ask 'suppose they had been Pacifics?'

The A2/1 was actually a Pacific based on the overall layout of the V2. It is often put forward as the best of the Thompson Pacifics, but it is rather difficult to say whether, in service, the A2/1 was better or worse than the V2, largely because no concerted trials were ever undertaken.

It is no part of our story to deal with Thompson's conversions of Gresley's locomotives, though one must comment on the very awkward appearance that resulted

from a near-fanatical insistence on equal length connecting rods whilst adopting a divided drive. In addition, the austere lines of the running board looked ugly against the gorgeous sweeps of the Gresley reverse curves. There were good reasons for this however; those curves added appreciably to the work involved and at the time unnecessary work was best avoided.

A more serious consequence followed Thompson's change of policy. The new CME had taken a very firm public stand on conjugated valve gear; unfortunately, this meant that he had to show up its defects, and thereafter everyone on the locomotive side had a perfect excuse for any shortcomings, although under the

conditions after 1941, there were plenty of other reasons why maintenance suffered.

The V2s were badly hit. They were a second rank locomotive and hence if things had to be rushed, they were the locomotives that got the quick treatment. There is no doubt that many were allowed to get into a sorry state, and that faults were offered to the CME as further proof that Gresley's machines were very difficult to keep in good working order. Thompson was in an impossible situation; he could not lay down a directive that they should be maintained properly even though, under his management at Darlington, they had been correctly built and maintained.

Below: The summer-only up *Scarborough Flyer* in September 1960, passing York, headed by Green Arrow No 60800, originally LNER No 4771.
Right: Green Arrow No 4771 after restoration to its original condition on Great Western territory at Didcot.
Original *Green Arrow* No 4771 on display at New Barnet when new in 1937.
Below left: Preserved Green Arrow No 4771 at Steamtown Museum in August 1974.

Post-war revival

Britain's railways emerged from the trauma of the Second World War in a worse condition than any of the other combatants' systems. Superficially, they seemed in reasonable condition, for they had escaped the spectacular havoc that occurred when the Allied and Russian armies rolled across Europe; but in 1940 and 1941 they were severely pounded by the Luftwaffe and had subsequently been used intensively to provide logistic back-up for the invasion of Europe and, of course, the massive strategic bombing of Germany carried out from 1943 onwards.

The railway system was able to take the load with ease, and had normal standards of track maintenance and replacement been maintained, and resources applied to what were arbitrarily regarded as 'non-essential' items such as passenger coaches, then there would have been little to criticise. However, the decision was taken, probably without much debate, to mortgage the future. In 1946 the British railway system, which in 1939 had been a beautifully conceived, well-maintained machine, had been battered into what a Labour politician was shortly to describe as a sorry bag of assets.

Some political comment is needed at this stage, for many of the post-war problems arose from well-meant but misapplied interference by Parliament. In the case of the railways, the interference was critical. A Labour Government was returned in the first post-war election and one of its priorities was the nationalisation of the railways. The various railway Boards were immediately hamstrung, for they were unwilling to invest large sums in the system when that investment would be against the interests of

their shareholders. At the same time, the State was clearly not going to spend public money improving a privately owned asset.

This is where the British railway system lost out. In Europe, sections of the various railway systems had been wrecked, and even the least perceptive voter realised something had to be done. Once given the go-ahead, European civil engineers were able to initiate wholesale renewals of routes.

Let us suppose that in 1944, as a last desperate effort, the Germans had launched an air attack on Britain, and as a result the Potters Bar tunnels were in danger of imminent collapse and two spans of the Welwyn viaduct severely weakened so that all East Coast traffic had to travel via the Hatfield loop. There would have been no question of making do; the line would have been virtually rebuilt, because it would have made sense to re-lay all the track whilst the route was out of action.

Although this is intended to set the scene, it has particular relevance to the V2 story. The LNER moved into the post-war period with a line that had been neglected and a collection of locomotives badly in need of overhaul. Fortunately, thanks to Gresley's initial policy, and Thompson's subsequent sound husbandry, the locomotive potential was good. There was virtually the full collection of Gresley heavyweights, of which the 184 relatively modern V2s formed an important part. There were the Thompson Pacifics, the excellent Thompson B1s and the many Thompson rebuilds that had given an extension of life to old but basically sound designs.

Although the V2 was conceived as a fast freight locomo-

tive, it is clear that, in this context, fast means precisely that; the locomotives were capable of very high speeds. They had been shown, both in peace and war, to be capable of doing almost the same work as the Pacifics and so in the immediate post-war period they were used mainly on passenger trains. This made good sense, for the concept of fast parcels and freight services had been a casualty of war, and in the post-war period, alas, the commercial department seemed unable or unwilling to make the effort to fight off road competition in the only practical fashion available, by providing a better, guaranteed delivery.

All went well until, during 1946, there were two derailments at Hatfield. The prime cause of both was that the track was in an abominable condition, and quite unsuited for the speeds permitted, although by GNR main line standards these were extremely low. By coincidence, both locomotives involved happened to be V2s.

Fortunately, neither derailment was serious in the popular sense; no one was killed and hardly anyone was injured. There was a slight element of luck involved, but subsequent experience with medium and high speed derailments underline the great advantage of one of Gresley's earliest design changes, the use of buckeye couplings on the early East Coast joint stock, and its subsequent use on all major LNER coaching rakes. The derailments took place at around 60 mph (96.5 km/h); several coaches left the track, but the trains did not jack-knife, the coaches did not telescope. They remained more or less upright with the bodies intact and, to paraphrase Ian Fleming, the passengers were shaken but not smashed.

In fact, these two derailments were so unspectacular that they have never been included in any of the many excellent and exhaustive accounts of railway accidents. At best, they are given a couple of paragraphs. This emphasises the fallacy of judging accidents by the butcher's bill; they had far-reaching consequences.

To paraphrase Oscar Wilde, to have one accident in a particular location involving a particular class of locomotive could be a misfortune; to have two such accidents in a short time smacks of carelessness. The press were not slow to pick this up.

There is a certain amount of irony involved. When, the Southern Railway's 'River' class 2-6-4 tanks were similarly involved in spectacular derailments at speed, the locomotive's stability was checked by high speed runs on the East Coast line, over this particular stretch. The conclusions were that although the 'Rivers' were quite stable on good tracks, on the sort of track common on much of the Southern at that time, they were apt to roll, setting up surges in the side tanks with disastrous results. They were rebuilt as tender locomotives and, without the hazard of oscillating water, were able to maintain high speeds over less than perfect track with complete safety, the leading pony truck notwithstanding.

However, anyone who had ever operated a model railway was aware that a locomotive fitted with a leading pony truck is more liable to derail than one fitted with a leading bogie — if we are talking of small scale models. This is because in 1946 no manufacturer considered it necessary to provide any form of side control, and only in the case of a leading bogie was a little vertical springing involved. In fact, a lot of model locomotives will run quite happily with the leading and trailing wheels removed, since some 80 per cent of the weight is carried by the driving wheels. Untroubled by civil engineering restrictions, a model

locomotive engineer can use axle loads approaching the equivalent of 100 tons per axle! Whilst this is totally irrelevant to full-sized locomotives it is important to remember that most people who are seriously interested in railway matters have owned a model railway at some time in their lives.

It was easy to take all these facts together, plus the fact that production of the class was stopped and the last four were turned out as Pacifics; put two and two together to produce twenty two! The 'Green Arrows' were freight engines — the adjective 'express' being conveniently forgotten — they had been pressed into express passenger service as a wartime expedient, was it not a scandal, etc etc.

To be fair to the press, both readers and editors expect their 'railway correspondent' to produce an answer before the accident inspectors have collected together the whole of the evidence or drawn any conclusions from their findings. Railwaymen in any position of authority tend to be tight-lipped at such times since the matter is technically sub judice and premature statements to the press can prejudice the outcome of the inquiry. In this instance, even without official leaks, popular opinion had its effects, for the

V2s were critically examined.

Before we go on to this, two aspects of the derailments need to be mentioned. The first is that the inquiry blamed the track, which was in very bad condition. This was accepted by the civil engineers from the outset, and not only were speed restrictions re-examined and in certain cases reduced still further, but much more to the point, the need to accelerate the improvement programme was brought home to everyone concerned. The second, far more important aspect was the confirmation of the value of the buckeye coupling on high speed passenger trains as a valuable second line of defence. It is not too far-fetched to suggest that the happy consequence of two potentially disastrous high speed derailments was that the adoption of buckeye couplings on future British Railways standard coaches was made certain. In many subsequent accidents the death toll has been either reduced or eliminated completely because the coaches did not part company and were thus less subject to damage. At the time of writing a spectacular derailment has occurred at Paddington, happily accompanied by minimal casual-

BR No 60808, formerly LNER V.2 No 4779, in unclean form at Thornaby Shed in April 1961.

ties and no loss of life. The immediate television reports spoke of the value of the 'new' buckeye couplings, which suggests again that the media still rely on reporters whose knowledge of railways is largely limited to models.

However, it was officially decided that the swing-link suspension of the Gresley pony truck was suspect, that spring control was better and the entire class was suitably modified. To the lay mind this sounds reasonable; there is a feeling that swing links can just move wideways and, since there are odd clanks and crashes when some wear has occurred in the pins, it seems reasonable that a spring, combined with inclined planes, is preferable.

This is a fallacy. The underlying principle of swing-link suspension is to restrain the side movement of the pony truck by fractionally lifting the support. In other words to apply the same principle as an inclined slide control, but to use rigid links and easily renewed pivot pins in place of a large flat surface, which is subject to wear and very easily affected by dirt. Even when some degree of slackness is present in the pins, the basic constraint is not altered in quality. However, slackness in the pivots does leave a small side movement without

effective control, and under the Thompson regime the swing-links, like the conjugated valve gear, were regarded as examples of Gresley fussiness, and were considered to be difficult to maintain. Hence on some locomotives, they were in a very poor state, and although not the primary cause of the derailment, they were a contributory factor.

It is quite clear that the swing-links could have been brought back into tip-top condition had anyone in authority admitted that the design had proved quite reliable in service, and that sloppy maintenance and unwise extension of essential repairs, was the root problem. A lot, however, would have depended on just how badly the pintles of the links had been distorted by the general bashing they had received. Under prevailing conditions, the replacement by a different design made good sense. It was a complete answer to critics and the new arrangement sounded better to the lay enthusiasts. Under the Thompson regime the swing-links had been labelled as difficult to maintain, and such a reputation is difficult to loose. Most important of all, it is a long established principle in engineering maintenance that whenever complex components show a general tendency to perform badly after

several years of arduous service, it is cheaper to throw the whole thing on the scrapheap and fit a new unit. At the same time the design can be modified in the light of experience, and undoubtedly it was this, rather than any half-mythical feud, that led to the renewal.

Once the tracks began to get back to their pre-war condition, and the locomotives received the badly-needed major overhauls necessary after their arduous wartime duties, the V2s began to regain their pre-war sparkle. Regrettably, outside factors prevented the full glories returning, for the railways were not only short of experienced men, but there was not the same enthusiasm from above. So observers were treated to an equal number of dull, lack-lustre runs as they were enthused by fine performances. Even though the schedules had improved, they were still well below pre-war levels and there was a general acceptance of poor-quality work which was very demoralising. Matters were made more complicated by the Government's attitude, for in addition to the threatened nationalisation, austerity was the order of the day.

BR No 60983 with the first Creston tender in 1953 at York Shed, giving a clear view of the valve gear and motion.

The final years

In his personal account of his work at Swindon, K. J. Cook briefly mentions his transfer to Darlington in British Railways days. Modestly, he suggests that it was a waste of time and instances only one development, the fitting of a copper cap to the chimney of a V2.

Few students of latter day British steam practice will agree. His move, together with others made about the time, was part of a careful plan developed by R. A. Riddles and his close associates, E. S. Cox and R. C. Bond. As young engineers on the new LMS, they had seen how the internecine battles between Crewe and Derby, with Horwich and Cowlairs joining in out of sheer devilment, had hamstrung progress in the locomotive department until an outsider was brought in to settle the argument for once and for all. Doubtless, as keen, ambitious young men will do, they discussed the problems and decided what they would have done in the circumstances. Unlike most people in this position, they got their chance, and to their eternal credit, they effectively squashed the natural tendency of the existing works to push their little quirks by the simple process of moving the top men around. The policy not only worked, but with Smeddle at Swindon and Cook at Darlington, it paid handsomely.

One of the hazards of engineering practice is that a particular design can acquire a reputation for unreliability. Once the men on the shop floor have it firmly in their minds that a particular arrangement is no good, it is doomed. As has been shown, from 1941 onwards certain features of Gresley practice were also condemned from on high. Where such features involved

extra work, or even the appearance of extra work, by the maintenance engineers, that was enough.

Worse than this, even the supporters of the conjugated gear were aware of its problems, and that the centre engine could develop more than its rated horsepower as a result. So when big ends gave trouble, there was a ready-made excuse to hand, and it has long been accepted that the prime cause of the big end troubles on the more powerful Gresley locomotives was the inherent faults of conjugated valve gear.

In his book *Swindon Steam* K. J. Cook devotes an entire chapter to the subject of big ends, and he relates how, after a few years in service, the GWR 'Kings' began to exhibit an alarming tendency to show signs of heating of the big ends. There was no convenient valve gear to blame, no tendency for the trouble to be concentrated on one bearing more than others, and so it was not possible to regard the problem — which, as with the Gresley machines, was intermittent in nature — to be regarded as part of the nature of the beast.

A close inspection of the affected bearings suggested that the trouble was caused by a partial breakdown in lubrication, and so this line of investigation was taken up. The older methods of bearing lubrication were beginning to come under close scrutiny, for as oil technology improved, it became increasingly clear that there could be equally useful improvements if the early hit-and-miss systems of lubrication could be brought from the eighteenth into the twentieth century.

Of course, in automative engineering, improved bearing

lubrication was well-established, and even though the crankshafts revolved in an oil chamber, the idea that you could splash the oil about and hope enough of it finished up in the bearings was no longer regarded as good enough — mainly because such arrangements usually produced a flurry of disintegrating big end bearing shells. Forced lubrication was now standard practice in all modern internal combustion engines.

However, applying such techniques to the much larger bearings of a reciprocating steam locomotive proved rather more difficult, so Swindon looked elsewhere. The solution proved to be remarkably simple in practice but extremely sophisticated in concept.

A felt pad was introduced across the bearing, with the idea of providing a continuous supply of oil at the point needed. This replaced the traditional arrangement of oil grooves, which were cut by hand in the bush according to arcane patterns handed down by successive fitters. At the same time the old practice of bedding the bush in by hand was abandoned, and bronze liners were eliminated in favour of a continuous whitemetal bearing. The whitemetal was given a very careful final cut with a broad-faced tool to provide an extremely smooth, highly-polished surface which was absolutely true. The basic technique was not new, it has been known since the earliest days of precision boring. At the same time, crankpins could easily be finished true, and then measured accurately so that the bushes could be manufactured with precisely the requisite clearance, which was virtually the traditional rule of thumb 'one thou per inch of bearing diameter'.

There was nothing revolutionary about this, but the important point is that the laboratories had just worked out in detail why oil prevents a bearing seizing, and realised that a film two molecules thick was enough, providing it could be maintained. It was also understood that to maintain this thin film at the point of maximum pressure an even bearing surface was needed so that the oil could be gently squeezed over the whole of the bearing. Naturally, it took a lot more than this to get the arrangement perfected, and several configurations of felt pad were tried until the final arrangement — in practice the least complicated — was decided upon. The hair on the felt also had to run in the right direction.

There remained one detail to attend to, the actual oil supply. From the earliest days of locomotive engineering, the method used had been the oil well, a large reservoir at the top of the bearing with a vertical pipe in the centre. worsted wick was placed in the centre pipe, and allowed to trail in the oil, thus regulating the flow. Not only was this traditional, but like the obsolete concept of oil grooves, all enginemen had their pet arrangements of wicks, and on top of shed practice, personal variations were added. The number of strands, the precise fixing of the supporting wire, the length, and any other detail that seemed a promising line of trial and error, formed part of the mystique. Despite the fact that a system that worked well with such a variety of methods might be open to question, it seemed that wicks did no actual harm and the drivers enjoyed themselves.

It is not clear how the idea came to be accepted that it was possible to leave wicks out altogether. Whilst a wick has its value on a fixed bearing, the big end of a locomotive is whirling round very rapidly, and the oil in the reservoir is swilling around. All the wick does is to slow down its passage to the bearing. At rest, the wick ensures a good supply to the bearing, but the fully-saturated felt pad is much more effective. So the wick was omitted, and a restrictor plug placed in the feed pipe. This does not restrict the flow of oil, for the felt pad serves to meter the supply to the bearing. Its function is to place a restriction on the engineman, and stop him from inserting a wick which in this type of bearing is a definite hazard. Cook suggests that a better name could have been found, but even so it was very diplomatic for a direct reference to its real purpose would have infuriated the engineman, and could have led to its surreptitious removal.

The new technique was beautiful both in its simplicity and sophistication. It not only worked, but actually pleased everyone concerned. The machine shops were delighted as they were given the opportunity of producing one of their specialities, a near perfect surface made by simple machining. The fitters in the erecting shops were delighted because the men in the machine shops no longer expected them to produce by hard labour what ought to have been done by machine. The drivers discovered that preparation was simplified and they no longer had the niggling fear that they might not have put the wick in correctly whilst scrabbling about under the engine, reaching up over the big end. Cook brought the technique to Darlington where they tried it, pronounced it good, and overheated big ends became a thing of the past.

Cook introduced another development, the optical lining-up. Carl Zeiss of Jena, had produced an optical collimator that greatly simplified the business of getting the bearings and cylinders in precisely the right place. All German railway workshops collected a set, but alone of British Railways, the GWR followed suit. Cook was particularly involved with its installation and development and, in his new works, missed it greatly. By now Jena was in East Germany and there was no chance to order another set, but a British manufacturer exhibited a similar device in the Machine Tool Exhibition of 1952, and investigation showed that the home grown product was slightly superior.

These two developments greatly improved the overall performance of all locomotives shopped at Doncaster. Cook had no prejudice against Gresley practice, indeed, in his presidential address to the Institution of Locomotive Engineers he specifically bracketed his name with that of Churchward and from a Swindon trained engineer, there can be no higher praise. He also emphasised cross-fertilisation of ideas.

The final years of steam operation of British Railways were exceptional, largely due to this cross fertilisation of ideas and techniques. By a happy chance, each of the major works had, in the thirties and before, concentrated on particular aspects of the steam locomotive, partly to improve its efficiency but mainly to improve its reliability. The nature of a railway, a single line of guide/support rails to carry vehicles along a fixed route, imposes a high premium of reliability. If a locomotive breaks down it affects not only the train it is hauling, but every train behind it as well. Over the years various shifts and stratagems to permit it to limp home with half its mechanism propped up with wood or tied up with wire and string had been devised, but the problem now was to discover how to stop it breaking down in the first place.

By 1948, most of the major faults had been identified and a simple, effective cure discovered. The trouble was that no one railway seemed to know them all, but after the heads of departments had been shifted around,

'Up' Fitted Freight near Hadley Wood in July 1959, hauled by V.2 No 60871, formerly LNER No 4842.

the various ideas became spread about. Cox has explained how, when the BR standard steam locomotives were designed, an important parameter was reliability, and in each case the fittings were based on the design which had been shown to give least trouble in service. In a similar fashion, any little fitting which was prone to give trouble was replaced with one that was more predictable in its behaviour.

This had an important bearing on locomotive performance. On the one hand it encouraged the enginemen to work their locomotives hard, in the knowledge that nothing was likely to go wrong. This encouraged the timetable department to shave minutes off the schedules, since there were fewer lame ducks about. It also encouraged the first moves

towards the modern concept of Inter-City service, a regular hourly or two hourly, train between two major points, with a fixed pattern of stops. It is not fully appreciated that there is nothing very original in the idea, its value was appreciated well before the turn of the century.

What was needed was greater reliability in motive power.

Unfortunately, this took something out of the innocent pleasures of the student of locomotive performance, since there were fewer examples of exceptional running to record. Not only were schedules laid down for the normal working of the class, but there were fewer cases where a major breakdown led to a smaller locomotive being commandeered.

The Eastern and North Eastern regions, together with those parts

of the Scottish region that had formed part of the LNER, had for this work a large number of modern locomotives suitable for express work:

Class		Number in class
W1	4-6-4	1
A1	4-6-2	50
A2	4-6-2	40
A3	4-6-2	78
A4	4-6-2	34
V2	2-6-2	184

With over 47 per cent being V2s, the importance of the class cannot be overstated. Unfortunately there were a number of machines that were definitely below par. A V2 in good order was an excellent machine, but many were out of condition. In

No 60835 class V.2 in October 1963 at Gleneagles with the up Grampian Express.

No. 60847, *St. Peter's School, York*, leaves home past its shed in September 1959. *Above*: Princes Street Gardens, Edinburgh, with No 60818 taking the 13.18 ex-Edinburgh to Crail.

part, the conjugated gear could be blamed for some of the faults, but not for indifferent steaming and excessively high coal consumption. One of the black sheep, No 60845, was sent to Swindon for a thorough test. It is ironic that this was done here rather than at Derby, the plant Sir Nigel Gresley had so assiduously promoted, but in the event the only

Gresley locomotive to run on the rollers at Derby was 'Sir Nigel Gresley', and then purely as a ceremonial opening gesture.

The Swindon test results have to be seen in relation to the circumstances; the subject was a poor locomotive to begin with. It is true that it had been sent in an overhauled condition, but even so the results were still disappointing.

But the tests also showed up several good points. The boiler itself came out remarkably well with an extremely high efficiency and, equally important, an excellent overall performance. Even at the maximum output the efficiency was comparable to any other British boiler, and at its optimum it was well in advance of the majority. Despite its conjugated gear, the front end was also shown to be good, particularly at higher speeds, and at minimum steam consumption rates the combination of boiler and front end produced the highest figures for efficiency of any British locomotive tested to that date. So much for the faults of conjugation! Unfortunately, it also showed that the efficiency dropped off considerably when the locomotive was exerting high power at low speeds, and that in its current form it was restricted in the smokebox. This was not part of the original design, but was the result of adding LMS pattern self-cleaning baffles. These saved a good deal of work in the sheds, but were prone to play havoc with the steaming capabilities if they were not carefully proportioned.

This was one reason why Swindon was chosen for the tests rather than Derby, for by now the works had gained an enviable reputation for engine doctoring. Under S. A. Ell, theory was married to the traditional dodges practised for over a century by astute enginemen, to create a fund of knowledge concerning locomotive front ends that enabled them in almost every case to take an indifferent locomotive and improve its performance out of all recognition. The V2 was accordingly 'breathed on' and the improved draughting was applied piecemeal to the class.

Although under certain types of working coal consumption increased, the result was a much more reliable locomotive, capable of holding its own in traffic. The tests, however, only revealed what had long been appreciated from performance on the road, that V2s were at their best when set to work lighter trains at high speeds.

The V2s did not, however, get the full benefit of double blast-pipes. One reason undoubtedly was that they were a bit too far down the line to get the treatment for by the time the initial tests were undertaken, the end of steam was in sight. A more cogent reason is indicated in the test results.

The V2s were part of Gresley's second generation of locomotives. It is clear that the boiler was an excellent one and, in its original condition, the front end matched. The introduction of self-cleaning screens did little to help, but Swindon's relatively simple modifications to the proportion of the various fittings inside the smokebox produced a well-balanced machine, and whereas the Pacifics benefitted in a startling manner from the provision of a double blastpipe, the difference between a normal V2 and a double blastpipe version was minimal. Only with the full Kylchap arrangement was there any significant difference. With steam on the way out, there was no point in spending additional money on the class.

However, there were to be some final flings. On a railtour, a V2 clocked 82 mph (132 km/h), and sustained a steady 75 mph (120 km/h) between Darlington and York with a load of nine coaches. This was an excellent piece of work, but under very special conditions. Locomen prefer to demonstrate their skill in front of an appreciative audience, and one of the reasons railtours were so popular at the time was that one could generally bank on a sprightly run, with the consolation that on other days there would be an interesting failure. Either way there was ample material to discuss afterwards.

To the end of their days the V2s were used on fitted freights, and generally they were preferred for this duty to anything else. This ensured that many of their best performances remained un-honoured and unsung, since observers on freight trains are few and far between. It seems, moreover, that they were rather better in their final days than the express classes they worked with and in general were preferred by the drivers.

The early days of diesels gave them a choice to shine. It has to be said that before the engine-man became fully familiar with the new locomotives, diesels were prone to failure. This was largely because the men could not distinguish between the rattles that denoted a loose housing and those that heralded a defect in the engines. As a result, some locomotives were taken off because one of the hatch fastenings was a little loose, whilst others broke down because what the driver assumed was a loose hatch clip turned out to be a big end. So, steam had the chance to substitute and here the Kylchap-fitted V2s at Peterborough proved excellent substitutes. One of the best performances from a V2 occurred when a Deltic failed on the down 'West Riding' and one of the Peterborough Kylchap-fitted V2s took over the 11 coach train and put up a highly creditable performance. It must be admitted, however, that 11 coaches, whilst a reasonable load for a V2 in good condition, was quite light for the super-powerful Deltics.

A lightly-loaded V.2 with only six coaches. This is No 60869 (LNER No 4840) on a down Cambridge train at Brookmans Park in September 1958.

The wrong pedigree

One comment frequently made about the 'Green Arrows' is that there was too much race-horse in their pedigree and not enough cart-horse. It is a very attractive simile, particularly in view of the fact that A3 Pacifics were named after race-horses, and the V2 boiler was derived from that source. Unfortunately, it misses the point.

The story of the V2 is confused by two quite adventitious factors. The first is that the boiler used the firebox and, presumably, the flanging plates of the A3 boiler, and therefore the locomotive was a cut-down Pacific. The second is that there was a proposal for an improved K3, and that a peculiar articulated locomotive was investigated. The implication that this was a step on the road to the V2 exists in B. Spencer's paper on Gresley locomotives, but this is solely by association. All he actually said was that the design was under active consideration at the same time.

The 'Green Arrows' have been

criticised because, unlike the 4-6-0 mixed-traffic machines, they were far better hauling relatively light loads at high speeds than tackling heavy loads at low speeds, in that to undertake hard collar work increased fuel consumption and reduced the thermal efficiency of the locomotive. Furthermore, their axle loading and overall length barred them from certain extremities of the system. On these grounds, they were not an economical go-anywhere, do-anything locomotive.

However, if we look instead at the stated purpose of the machine, we discover that it was brought out to work fast fitted freights and supplement the Pacifics on certain passenger duties. A fast fitted freight is generally a relatively light load, and runs at high speed, which is precisely the sort of work a V2 would perform effectively and economically. The class was also extremely effective on passenger work, and it is irrelevant that it

used a little more coal in certain circumstances. How many motorists consider the thermal efficiency of their car, or attempt to drive at the most economical cruising speed at all times?

In short, the V2s were built to perform a specific task. All available records show that they performed that task superbly and were capable of coping admirably with a wide variety of tasks forced on them by circumstances that were not even contemplated during the design stage.

However, a careful study of the locomotive's main characteristics reveals an extremely intriguing possibility. Although the origins owed a lot to the need for an improved K3, the most important details of the design — the mono-bloc cylinders and the driving wheels — are common to the P2 2-8-2. The suggestion put forward here is that the V2s were part of Gresley's second generation of locomotives.

The Pacifics, the 2-8-0s and the 2-6-0s were initially conceived around 1914, although it was not until later that the concept was finalised. The object, brilliantly executed, was to provide a large number of powerful

locomotives fully able to handle the traffic of the immediately foreseeable future. The A4s, superb as they were, represent the maximum possible within that basic concept.

It is normal for a locomotive designer to look ahead, to anticipate what will be needed. During the 1930s and on into the 1940s, all railways in Britain were looking at the next generation. Gresley did more, he actually built three of the future locomotives, his second generation locomotives.

An important piece of evidence that suggests that Gresley was actively contemplating new locomotives was his active lobbying for a comprehensive test plant. Of course, it is great fun to run tests of locomotives, but the cost involved and the investment in test gear is only justified if the object is to see what improvements can be made. So far as checks on existing locomotives were concerned, dynamometer trials, coupled with careful study of operating statistics, are perfectly adequate.

The first design was, of course, the P2. This broke away from the original concept by adopting a monobloc cylinder casting. Regardless of whether the single casting was preferable to three separate units bolted together, the arrangement materially reduced the loading on the frames, and made for a more rigid chassis. No doubt some flexing had been noted on the existing locomotives. There was also the eight-coupled wheelbase, still comparatively rare in Europe on high speed locomotives. The small P2 class provided a useful test bed for future development of the projected 4-8-2, not merely in the obvious matter of the chassis, but on the question of firing the higher powered locomotives to come.

It is not too fanciful to suggest that the class was set to work over an exceptionally sinuous

Above: Green Arrow, being restored to its original condition in November 1962.

Class V.2 No 60967 being overhauled at Darlington Works in April 1967.

Right: Locomotive interchange, not possible in 1925. V.2 No 60845 (formerly LNER No 4816) on test at Swindon in 1953.

route primarily to find out, under adverse conditions, what effect an eight-coupled chassis would have in service. With both these and the A4s there was an opportunity to test whether or not firemen could be encouraged to shovel coal into the firebox at exceptional rates. There have been many assessments of the power limitations of a design, but in the final analysis, the power output of a hand-stoked, coal-fired locomotive is the willingness of the fireman to shovel coal.

The V2 shares many points in common with the P2s, as has been shown. It was primarily built to work fitted freights, and was not a normal mixed-traffic engine. It is clear that the idea of an 'enlarged K3' was squashed largely because the K3 was just about as big a locomotive as could be built within the length limitations. A longer locomotive

could not fit the turntables, and so a larger locomotive did not need to meet the weight limitations imposed by the very routes which had not been re-equipped with larger turntables. It might just as well take advantage of the weight limits set for the majority of the main lines.

It can be argued that, but for the wartime restrictions that stopped the construction of passenger locomotives, fewer V2s would have been built. That is pure speculation, but we have other indications of what was planned.

There were the two 'Bantam Cocks', an extremely intriguing design. They have been described as Rolls Royces sent to do the work of a Ford. This is a facile and totally incorrect statement. They bore the same relationship

to existing secondary line locomotives as the Churchward 45XX class of 2-6-2 tank bore to the saddle tank locomotives they replaced. To use a motoring analogy, they represented the difference between a pre-war Ford and its current equivalent. In other words, it was a brilliant leap forward, an imaginative machine that could have done

what the V2s were intended to do had it been given a proper chance — provide a challenge to the road competition on the secondary services.

In two classes, Gresley used a wide firebox boiler on locomotives where, until then, narrow fireboxes had been the rule. There is little doubt that, under post-war conditions, wide fire-

Gresley's Second Generation Locomotives

Class	Wheel arrangement	Duties
???	4-8-2	Projected express passenger
P2	*2-8-2*	*Express passenger*
V2	*2-6-2*	*Express freight, passenger*
V4	*2-6-2*	*Secondary services*
?	2-6-4T	Local and suburban. Projected
?	2-8-2	Hypothetical heavy freight

Italicised classes were built.

boxes were an asset, for they were better at coping with poor coal and, although when pressed they might show lower thermal efficiencies, when we look at railway operation in an overall sense, a locomotive which can be guaranteed to haul its train to time at the expense of a little extra fuel is preferable to one which on a good day burns less coal, but on a bad day refuses to burn anything!

There are still two other locomotives to consider. The first is an intriguing proposal for a 2-6-4 tank with a wide firebox — more or less a tank version of the V4, but with only two cylinders to provide room for a well tank. Just how this project might have ended up is a matter for debate, but again it reveals the leaning towards a wide firebox.

Finally, there is the projected 4-8-2. This locomotive again only reached the investigatory stage, but it had intriguing potential. One point that would have created some difficulty is the question of ashpan capacity. Cox has pointed out that on the LMS the probability of a 4-6-4 was being explored since experience with the Stanier Pacifics suggested that, on the run to Glasgow, the main problem would be holding the ash generated. So, the 4-8-2 might have become a 4-8-4, or possibly gone over to oil firing.

The table of second generation Gresley locomotives includes a completely hypothetical heavy freight 2-8-2, postulating the lengthening of goods loops on the main line to permit 120 wagon trains, or some other variation — high capacity bogie hopper wagons for example, that would enable heavier coal trains to be accepted.

It was not to be. The war came, and Gresley died in office, but enough was done to show the outlines of a range of locomotives that could have established Gresley as the greatest

locomotive engineer of all time. Some people already maintain this, but even they will admit that if his designs had been given a fair chance, they would not have to argue so vehemently. Of course, much of the Gresley style depended on conditions that were swept away in World War II and a great deal of criticism is levelled against arrangements that were less than satisfactory where maintenance was allowed to slide.

When we consider the notorious valve gear, it seems clear that much of the blame for over-riding of the valve lay, not with the design, but in the execution of the gear itself. However, the piston valve reciprocating steam engine is extremely tolerant, and the main effect of the slop was to produce a range of interesting noises. This had the side effect of preventing Doncaster or Darlington independently coming up with the realisation that there were better ways of lubricating a big end bearing than those currently in vogue. It is perhaps important to reflect that although there are many tales about the failure of big ends, nothing is said of the fact that such failures were extremely rare.

An equally important factor that must be considered is that

whereas it was thought necessary to spend a great deal of money to replace, in its entirety, O. V. Bulleid's chain-driven valve gear on the Merchant Navy and West Country Pacifics, it was not thought necessary to replace conjugated gear, even when the cylinders were renewed, even though this would only have amounted to adding an extra set of inside gear.

The other critical feature was the leading pony truck. This derailed on rough track, but before anyone jumps to the conclusion that it would have been all right if the locomotives had had a leading bogie, one has to remember that Black Fives also jumped the road when they encountered bad track and their bogie suspension was in poor condition.

However, the V2s have one interesting feature. One often speculates on what the performance would have been like had the locomotive been slightly different. In the A2/1 class we can see what a Pacific version of the V2s, with three independent sets of valve gears was like. The answer is that it was a very good locomotive, but it is doubtful that it was any better than the 'Green Arrows'.

Above: *Green Arrow* No 4771 preparing to haul "The Norfolkman" Special after restoration.
Left: The smokebox end of a Green Arrow, showing anti-vacuum valve and superheater header cover after restoration.
Right: Restored *Green Arrow* No 4771 in its original livery at Steamtown Museum in August 1974, alongside SNCF 'Chapelon' Pacific.

Green Arrow: Modelling Notes

It is remarkably easy to survey ready-to-run models of the V2 class — there aren't any!

For several years Lima listed a V2 as 'coming shortly'. This model only existed as a pre-production mock-up, and was to have been a very fine model indeed. For various reasons, it did not materialise, and it is highly unlikely that it will be revived in the foreseeable future. Although keen model operators can and frequently do point to the number of V2s working over Eastern Region metals, it is a sad fact that the LNER comes a poor fourth in popularity stakes, just beating the Southern by a whisker, and as the A3 and A4

class pacifics are much more popular with the general public, the manufacturers naturally concentrate on these.

A 4-mm scale cast whitemetal kit was produced by Nu Cast, and is available from time to time. Again, lack of widespread support means that it is not widely stocked.

Anyone wanting a complete ready-to-run model must place an order with one of the specialised manufacturers, who will undertake to produce a model, usually from a kit. Although this is fairly costly, and can take a long time, one can specify the exact condition, name and number required.

It looks simple enough to

convert a Hornby A3 'Flying Scotsman' and there is no better way than this of confirming the fact that the V2s were *not* cut down Pacifics. By the time the boiler has been shortened, the footplate completely reconstructed at a new level, and a new chassis incorporating extensively modified motion has been built, one discovers that the cab is different! Its quicker to scratchbuild.

For scratchbuilders, the excellent textbooks *Building Model Locomotives* by F. J. Roche and G. G. Templer and *Model Locomotive Construction in 4-mm scale* by Guy Williams should be consulted; both books are published by Ian Allan.

V2 'Green Arrow' class 2-6-2

Names

4771	Green Arrow
4780	The Snapper
	The East Yorkshire Regiment
	The Duke of York's Own
4806	The Green Howard
	Alexandra
	Princess of Wales's Own Yorkshire Regiment
4818	St Peter's School
	York AD 627
4831	Durham School
4843	The King's Own Yorkshire Light Infantry
4844	The Coldstreamer
60964	The Durham Light Infantry

Numbers

4771–5	Doncaster 1936	3641–54	Darlington 1942
4776–95	Darlington 1937	3655–60	Doncaster 1941
4796–4814	Darlington 1938	3661–4	Doncaster 1942
4815–42	Darlington 1939	3665–74	Darlington 1942
4843–46	Doncaster 1939	3675–90	Darlington 1943
4847–52	Doncaster 1940	3691–5	Darlington 1944
4853–62	Darlington 1939		
4863–88	Darlington 1940		
4889–98	Darlington 1941		
4899	Darlington 1942		
4771 was to have been 637			

Renumbering
First Scheme 1943
The class was to have been renumbered 700–883, but only 19
locomotives were actually renumbered: 701, 710, 711, 714, 718–22,
729, 733, 750, 762, 771, 795, 799, 805, 871.

Second scheme
4771–4899 became 800–938   3641–3695 became 939–983.
British Railways added 60,000 to all ex-LNER numbers.
First of class withdrawn 26 February 1962.
Class extinct 31 December 1966.
Original locomotive preserved in National Collection as 4771
'Green Arrow'.